Some reactions to this book:

"Motivation ... success ... happiness. They are on everyone's shopping list. By reading this book, they are all yours!"

- A Real Estate Salesperson

"A classic ... an advanced course on personal effectiveness which combines the art of human relations with the science of motivation ..."

- A High School Principal

"A creative, refreshing alternative to the predatory 'win-lose' philosophy most people practice."

- A Hospital Administrator

"G-M-C is powerful medicine! It instills that 'winning feeling' in people and helps increase individual self-esteem ..."

- A Practicing Pyschologist

"A beautiful book on how to give of yourself, to be part of something larger than yourself. It's in our self-interest to help one another."

- A Social Worker

First Printing
July 1987

REGISTERED WITH THE LIBRARY OF CONGRESS,
WASHINGTON, D.C.

ISBN: 0-9616385-0-8

FORWARD

Just why is motivation so important? It is important because employees with motivational problems cost organizations thousands, even millions, of dollars each year. Research shows that only 20% of employees can cause 100% of the grievances, 45% of the absences, 52% of the garnishments, 38% of the medical claims and 40% of all sick leave.

In a recent survey of 330 senior executives, it was estimated that the average office worker wastes 4 hours and 39 minutes of work time per week. In 1986, this cost USA employers $170 billion, a phenomenal drain on cash resources.

By reading this book and learning how to motivate people, you will save money, increase productivity, reduce the number of people who are late or absent, and cut down on employee turnover and wasted time. It provides down-to-earth techniques for solving typical employee morale problems, and increasing individual self-esteem.

Psychology can be defined as the scientific study of human behavior and mental thought processes. It involves all aspects of living, our happiness or sadness, our relationships, either good or bad, with family, friends, business associates and society in general. No endeavor, from building a marriage, raising children, communicating our ideas to others or selling a product is ever entirely separate from it.

I have great respect for motivational books that offer proven, practical advice. This is one of the very best I have found on superior human relations. Effective and loving relationships are important, as this book points out -- they account for 85% of all the happiness we can hope to have in our lifetime.

Dr. Staples is obviously a keen student of human nature. He is very adept at distilling essential truths down to their lowest common denominator, and embodying them in a narrative format that is both entertaining and educational.

His novel approach is full of sage advice, and designed to help people easily identify with this positive learning experience. The fruit of his labor is certainly our gain.

In the book, we are introduced to THE GREATEST MOTIVATIONAL CONCEPT IN THE WORLD, or G-M-C, a simple yet powerful formula for getting things done with and through other people. It takes the guesswork out of human relations, and helps us be in control. Like a card dealer playing with a stacked deck, we know the outcome of our personal encounters even before we start the game.

Dr. Staples tells it like it is, not how we would like it to be. Human nature cannot be changed to suit our wishes. We have to accept people the way they are and learn to work in harmony with them. Hence his challenge -- if you want to prosper, learn how to secure the cooperation of other people; otherwise, be prepared to fail time and time again. We all literally get our due in due course, whether we like it or not. The key is superior human relations -- they will either make you or break you.

Consider the human relations factor in an organizational setting. A common explanation why people who are competent at one level often fail when promoted to a higher level is Dr. Laurence Peter's famous "PETER PRINCIPLE." It suggests that because the higher level of responsibility demands different skills, people fail due to their lack of these new skills. The reason they fail, according to Dr. Peter, is because they have been promoted to their level of incompetence.

I believe Dr. Staples' book sheds some valuable light on this phenomenon.

When people are promoted in an organization, they become responsible, often for the first time, for supervising other people and monitoring their contribution to the organization's goals. But it cannot be expected that a salesperson promoted to manager due to his superior sales skills will know automatically how to manage and motivate a whole salesforce. Thus we see that as people progress higher and higher, superior human relations become more and more important because their influence permeates wider throughout the organization.

G-M-C is a sort of "PETER PRINCIPLE" in reverse -- those who consistently demonstrate an ability to achieve results with and through other people tend to be promoted to a level commensurate with their proven competence.

So, let's explore together ways to motivate people through superior human relations. You'll find the best way to do this involves increasing the self-esteem of others. But there is an additional, invaluable benefit you receive in the process -- when you increase the self-esteem of others, you automatically increase your own self-esteem as well. Clearly it is in our own self-interest to help one another.

- RAY DALY

THE SYMBOL

The Master Motivator's symbol -- the initials G-M-C enclosed by a circle -- is intended to remind us that human behavior is consistent and universal.

All races and nationalities are bound to conform to the laws of human nature.

TO MOTIVATE PEOPLE, YOU NEED THIS TOOL!

Managers, salespeople, parents and educators ... everyone wants to know how to motivate other people in one way or another.

G-M-C, THE GREATEST MOTIVATIONAL CONCEPT IN THE WORLD, provides the answer. It is the ultimate equation involving human relationships.

How people relate to one another in the end determines how successful they are with one another.

CONTENTS

1

INTRODUCTION

One of life's greatest challenges
and hopes is to create and
look forward to the next stage
of personal development.

In this brief story, you are exposed to techniques learned from the behavioral sciences about how people relate best with one another.

People need each other to get things done. Some methods of relating are more effective than others.

What is "best" is what works to get the desired results in a mutually beneficial way. Both participants in any encounter must gain in some way if either is to continue to benefit from the experience.

Effective human relationships are a primary goal in all social contact.

2

THE SEARCH

Both happiness and success
are a process and not
an end in themselves.

Once an ambitious young journalist set off in search of motivation and success. She was looking for a master motivator.

She wanted to meet one.

She wanted to become one.

She also wanted to write about one and report her experience to the world.

She was interested in motivation and its relationship to success, and wanted to be more in control of her life.

She knew this was an elusive goal. But she heard some had found the secret and was determined to find it for herself.

She felt life was too short not to live each day to the fullest.

She knew master motivators existed because many had become famous for this unique talent.

Some were wealthy and powerful, but not accessible.

Others were wealthy and accessible, but unable to explain their secret in simple terms.

She needed to find an articulate person, someone willing and able to explain his methods to others eager to learn.

Her search had taken her far and wide, to foreign lands and strange cultures.

She had travelled to many cities, large and small, and visited offices of every kind. She met motivators in universities, research centers, government agencies, military establishments and corporate board rooms, and talked to men and women of all ages, of all ranks, in various professions.

She was beginning to understand the wide range of methods people used to motivate other people.

But she was not impressed with what she found.

She met many motivators whose only goal was to win at all costs, and as they won, others they dealt with lost.

Some of their admirers thought they were very good motivators.

Many of their close associates thought they were not.

As the woman sat in each of these tough, "me-first" motivator's offices, she asked, "What kind of a motivator would you say you are?"

Their answers all had a familiar ring.

"I'm a loner -- I'm in the game to look out for number one," she was told. "If you don't look after yourself, no one else will. My bottom line is -- what's in it for me? My only interest is in coming out on top."

They all took great pride in their comments. Someone had to win, and they were determined it would be them.

The woman also met many "me-last" motivators, people who made sure other people always won at their expense.

Some of their admirers thought they were very good motivators.

Many of their close associates thought they were not.

As the woman sat and listened to these nice, passive people answer the same question, she heard them say, "I'm not as good as other people, so I know I must do what I can to help them. I'll only be hurt if I think of myself."

They also took great pride in their comments. Some people had to sacrifice themselves for the good of others, and it may as well be them.

But she was disturbed.

It was as though most motivators in the world were primarily interested in only one of two things -- in either taking all they could, while giving nothing in return, or giving all they could, while taking nothing in return.

Motivators who were interested only in taking were often labeled "intimidators" and "manipulators," while motivators who were interested only in giving were often labeled "capitulators."

The young woman thought each of these motivators -- the aggressive "intimidators" and the passive "capitulators" -- was only partially effective. It was like being only half a motivator, she thought, like a person with only one arm.

She returned home tired and distraught, but not discouraged.

She knew what she was looking for.

Successful human relations, she believed, was a two-way street. Both parties had to win if either was to win in any on-going productive relationship.

She had to find the mechanism, the dynamic concept to bring this about. She believed people should be "facilitators," each helping the other to feel good about himself.

The young woman continued to look everywhere for a master motivator.

Then one day she heard about an upcoming visit to her community by a remarkable gentleman, a renowned individual who toured major cities sharing his personal philosophy on how to get things done with and through other people.

He was famous for being the originator of "THE GREATEST MOTIVATIONAL CONCEPT IN THE WORLD."

He was widely respected as the consummate motivator and an enthusiastic speaker.

He was to address the local Chamber of Commerce.

At last! A master motivator.

She had to meet him.

She had to get an interview.

3

THE FIRST MEETING

Success, more and more,
is less and less a result
of individual effort.

The woman arranged to meet the gentleman at a reception the day before his speech.

When she arrived, she quickly recognized him in a crowd of people.

He stood out.

He was the center of attention.

After the reception, she approached him and introduced herself as the person who had asked for the interview.

"I'm pleased to meet a journalist interested in motivation," he responded. "Now, what can I do to help you?"

"I'd like to ask you some questions about how you go about motivating people," she stated.

"Of course. Fire away."

"Well, to begin, can you explain your fascination with motivation and why you think it is so important?"

"Yes. Many years ago, I asked myself -- How do you motivate people in this world to do things?

"You know, many a great thinker has considered this question, yet no consensus seems to have emerged. People today appear only slightly more enlightened and skilled in motivational concepts than they were fifty years ago. Then fear and force were the common practice.

"I'm convinced we have a long way to go in understanding human motivation, but the real fascinating part is to imagine just how much more we could all accomplish if we knew how to work more effectively together."

"But we have progressed in so many ways," she offered. "Look at all the new information and modern technology we have. Even our exploration of outer space."

"That's true. But at the same time it seems we have overlooked our inner space, that space between our ears! People today also tend to look for more complicated solutions to their everyday problems than they have to. This is the way of modern man."

"Then what is the answer?" she continued.

"I think we have to recognize that while many things are constantly changing, like human values and expectations, many things are not.

"Take human nature as a prime example," he suggested. "I believe it has not changed all that much over the years. People today are still goal-oriented beings with needs and desires looking for fulfillment."

"Interesting. But what does this have to do with motivation?" she questioned.

"To understand human nature is to understand people. Everyone is born with inherent needs and desires that determine why people say the things they say and do the things they do. Once you know their innermost needs and desires, and learn how to satisfy them, you have at your disposal the key to motivating people, to getting people to do the things you want them to do ... willingly."

*

HUMAN NATURE

HAS NOT CHANGED ALL THAT MUCH

OVER THE YEARS.

PEOPLE TODAY

ARE STILL GOAL-ORIENTED BEINGS

WITH NEEDS AND DESIRES

LOOKING FOR FULFILLMENT.

*

"Can you describe these inner motivators we all have?" she inquired.

"Of course. Some of the basic psychological needs and desires every normal, healthy person possesses include:

- a feeling of importance
- a sense of control over life
- recognition of effort
- opportunities for high achievement
- acceptance and approval
- a sense of belonging
- worthy goals and ideals
- financial independence
- dignity and self-respect
- love in its many forms

"In fact, I would call these ten factors the definition of what represents success for most people.

"We know motivation is important because achievement is seldom a solo performance. We all get things done with and through other people. This requires motivating people. The family, indeed every organization, exists only because it as a group of people can achieve more than what its individual members alone can accomplish. But to get people to do things, you have to know how to relate with them successfully."

"Just how do people relate to one another?" she probed.

"First, you must appreciate that people can relate only one-on-one," he pointed out. "You are always dealing with one individual or another. You never relate with 'people' -- it is only an abstract term.

"You must also realize that relating involves a great deal of give and take, and usually more of one, giving, or the other, taking, at any one point in time."

"But what dynamic forces are at play?" she inquired.

"The answer to that is simple," he said. "It is individual self-interest. People operate in accordance with how they perceive their self-interest is being served. Unconsciously, people are constantly checking to see if their inner needs are being satisfied.

"In any encounter, a person can quickly sense if you have his interests in mind or your own. That's why it's important to create a receptive, sharing atmosphere at the very beginning.

"Individual self-interest in the broadest sense is the purpose behind all human behavior."

"But I find relating to others is such a delicate, fluid process," she remarked. "There are so many pitfalls."

"Don't be deterred," he said encouragingly. "Many ego-related factors are at play that most people do not understand or are not fully aware of.

"Remember your ego is your most prized possession. People will do almost anything to protect their ego and are always trying to enhance it.

"Most people in life go around looking for one of two things. Either they are looking for what they want, and end up taking, or they are looking for what others need, and end up giving.

*

INDIVIDUAL SELF-

INTEREST IN THE BROADEST

SENSE IS THE PURPOSE BEHIND

ALL HUMAN BEHAVIOR.

*

"Unfortunately, the vast majority of people simply muddle through their personal encounters, but are always on the lookout for opportunities where only they can benefit from the experience.

"They practice the 'me first' rather than the 'me later' philosophy."

"Why are people so short-sighted?" she sighed.

"A very good question. It seems the desire to receive in people is instinctive, whereas the desire to give is something that has to be learned.

"During an encounter, people therefore tend to be overly preoccupied with satisfying their own ego-related needs on a subconscious level, forgetting they should be paying proper attention to the other person's needs on a conscious level. They incorrectly place their priority on their reason for the encounter and not on the needs of people. The result is often frustration, friction, even conflict."

"Are concepts of any kind relevant to the way we behave?" She was beginning to warm up to his way of thinking.

"Of course they are. Concepts necessarily influence our attitudes, and in turn our behavior and how we perceive our environment. The world we see is what we want it to be. We do have a choice. Concepts will work for us if we will work for them."

"I understand your philosophy evolves around the greatest motivational concept in the world. Just what is it?"

At this point, the gentleman's face lit up. It was as though he had been waiting for this moment all along.

"The greatest motivational concept in the world," he said, "is this:

In any relationship, you must first give others what they want before you can expect to receive what you want in return.

"It's the ultimate human equation. You will find that you can get everything you want in life if only you will help enough other people get what they want first. In other words, you must give in order to receive.

"Let me illustrate.

"The husband has to bring his wife flowers first, before he can expect more affection.

"The employee has to become more effective on the job first, before he can expect a pay raise.

"And the salesperson has to show interest in his customer first, before he can expect to make a sale.

"Unfortunately, most people practice this process in reverse.

"It's like the job applicant who wants to know what the company has to offer him before he's willing to discuss what qualifications he has to offer the company.

"Or the schoolteacher who wants a student to follow her lecture more attentively before she's willing to consider how she can make her presentation more interesting to him.

"All too often we begin by criticising other people before we consider what their problem is."

The young woman saw his point. "We all want something from our interpersonal relationships."

"Correct."

"And the effectiveness of all our relationships with others is critical to getting things done."

"Yes, that's it. Success lies in dealing with people more effectively. We all achieve our goals through other people and other people achieve their goals through us. There is no other way.

"We need to assume the burden of responsibility for each encounter, whether or not we are the initiator or recipient of the event. We control at least 50% of any relationship and 100% of our own behavior. Only by being in control of our daily encounters can we hope to influence the results in the most positive way, and in a way of potential benefit to both parties."

The young woman was intrigued. "Daily encounters. You really think they are that important?"

"They are absolutely critical to performance," he retorted. "Most people spend up to 70% of each day relating to other people in one way or another, for one reason or another. People need each other to achieve goals they cannot reach individually.

"Of course, you cannot and should not expect to win each and every encounter in a human relations sense -- there are difficult people in this world, but you should know in advance what the cause and effect factors are.

"Successful encounters mean successful days, successful days lead to successful weeks, and successful weeks translate into successful careers."

"But," she added, "someone has to get the ball rolling first -- by giving to the other person."

"Right. Consider the alternative. Ineffective relationships lead to divorce, runaway children, high employee turnover, and lost sales.

"Reflect on your own experience for just a moment. Haven't you noticed that the mark of a failure at human relations is the person who always blames other people for his problems? He never considers what **he** could do differently."

"So, to the extent we give others what they want, they will give us what we want in return. That's it?" she asked.

"Exactly. It's the key to getting people to do the things you want them to do, the central concept behind leading, guiding, motivating, selling, persuading, supervising or influencing others to follow you."

The gentleman paused to let the woman finish her notes.

He went on. "I believe successful human relations is the art of making other people feel good about themselves. By your behavior, you've got to convince them that you think they are important.

"With practice, we can develop the ability to influence other people effectively, and in the process learn how to satisfy our own inner needs. Such opportunities lie all around us, they are inherent in our everyday activities. We derive 85% of our happiness from effective and loving relationships.

"We know, for example, that cared-for staff in turn care for customers. And when you are able to relate your product or service to a customer's self-interest and sense of self-worth, you have created a receptive, buying attitude.

"You will achieve your goals more consistently when you make human nature work for you instead of against you."

"I see what you're saying," she said. "We get either positive or negative feedback in direct proportion to how well we are satisfying the needs of other people. And when we begin to receive positive feedback consistently, we know we are relating to others in accordance with their needs, allowing them to satisfy our needs in return. It's a natural cause and effect relationship. Can you give another example?"

*

YOU WILL

ACHIEVE YOUR GOALS

MORE CONSISTENTLY WHEN YOU

MAKE HUMAN

NATURE WORK FOR YOU

INSTEAD OF

AGAINST

YOU.

*

"Of course. Let's assume you want to achieve a particular goal in life in order to satisfy one of your needs. The result is very important to you -- yet to get what you want, you know you need the cooperation of another person. What do you do? You first carry out a 'needs' analysis by asking this important question -- 'Why should he help me?' In this way, you are beginning to identify what the other person wants in order to secure his support to move in the direction you desire. If you can find a way to give him what he wants from the process of following the path you have chosen, then you are far more likely to achieve your goal. When both parties are satisfied, you end up with a 'win-win' situation, which is the objective of any healthy relationship."

The young woman was taking in every word the master motivator was saying.

"So far, so good," she said. "But just what should I be giving to others to ensure their cooperation?"

"That's the fun part. You can choose between what you think they want, what you think they need, or even what you think they deserve! But never forget -- everyone wants to feel important.

"Although wants and needs can sometimes be the same, at other times they can be different.

"Let me give these examples," he continued, "and you'll see what I mean.

"A parent may find his child wants attention, when in fact he needs affection.

"An employer may find a staff member wants power and prestige, when in fact he needs recognition.

"And a car salesman may think a customer wants an expensive automobile, when in fact he needs reliable transportion.

"Now," he explained, "there is no simple formula that says you should satisfy all wants or all needs in every case. You must judge each situation on its own merits. Sometimes you should sell others on their wants and at other times sell them on their needs.

"The key to selling people on an idea is to determine the want or need that is relevant, then relate it to their self-interest.

"But please note that if all we satisfied in our society were needs, instead of wants and desires, our consumer-based economy would come to a grinding halt and we'd all be riding around on bicycles!"

"I wouldn't like that!" the young journalist exclaimed.

"You are saying we all have inherent needs for dignity, self-respect and a sense of self-importance, and although we ourselves seek these out in almost all we say and do, we often forget that others are doing the same thing."

"That's right," the gentleman replied.

"You see, we have a choice in how we go about relating to other people.

"We can act aggressively, take what we want and give nothing in return. For example, we can force others to do our bidding through intimidation. We can threaten to fire employees and physically abuse our children. But this method is neither enduring nor conducive to high performance. And our victims are always capable of retaliating against us in other ways.

"Or we can act timidly and passively, not asserting ourselves in any way, and hope others will be nice to us in return. This beggarly stance is also too one-sided and cannot be productive over time.

"Lastly, we can aim to give first then expect to receive over time, according to each other's needs. In this stance, both parties are more likely to benefit from the relationship.

"Experience shows that the person who believes he deserves nothing from this world but owes a lot will be on his way up. On the other hand, if he believes he owes nothing and deserves everything, he will be on his way down."

The gleam in the young woman's eyes showed she grasped his philosophy.

"We all will want something from other people," she concluded. "It all depends on the relationship.

"I can see that a parent will want obedience and affection from his children -- and they want understanding and security in return.

"An employer will want output, cooperation and loyalty from his employees -- and they will want compensation and recognition in return.

"A salesperson will want customers to buy his product or service -- and they will want respect and satisfaction in return.

"I think I'm becoming a master motivator myself!" she exclaimed.

"You certainly have grasped the basics," he replied.

"Each of us possesses valuable, intangible assets that other people are desperately in need of. We all have courtesy, praise, respect, empathy and goodwill in unlimited quantity -- to give! In this way, we acknowledge the importance of other people. They don't cost us anything and they can never be all used up. We all have this fortune to share!

"Few people appreciate this simple fact. We tend to hoard what we desperately seek. We hang on to these assets as though they were a finite resource we could run out of. At the same time, we go around purposely collecting and accumulating these same assets from others as much as possible in order to satisfy our own unquenchable thirst. We are all hungry for recognition."

The young woman breathed a sign of relief.

"Somehow I knew success was a two-way street," she said. "I just didn't understand the concept."

She then repeated out loud -- "We all receive by giving. It's so ironic!

"And the more we give, the more we receive. Only we have to make the investment first!

I see now that the greatest motivational concept in the world is infallible. In time, it will provide all the rewards we seek.

"Can we meet again?" she pleaded.

"I have so much more to learn."

4

THE SECOND MEETING

He who dreams and acts
on his dream is assured
of an exciting future.

She arranged to meet the master motivator again the following day.

In the meantime, she collected her thoughts on what he had said.

Motivation. What an elusive quality. Everyone wanted it but few knew what it was. And although we all recognized it in others, most of us didn't know how to acquire it for ourselves.

She decided to ask the master motivator these important questions.

"Good morning," he greeted her cheerfully at the hotel. "What would you like to discuss today?"

"Can we begin by explaining what motivation really is?"

"It would be a pleasure," he said. "Motivation is literally 'motive-in-action.' It is the internal drive within a person that is fueled by intense desire to achieve a particular goal. We are all motivated in life to do something or nothing, either a little or a lot. Motivation results from a conscious act to adopt an aspiration that interests us and whose attainment satisfies an inner need."

"How does motivation differ from ambition?" she wanted to know.

"Ambition is simply desire with no direction. Motivation, on the other hand, is present in a person who knows what he wants, is willing to go after it, and who has a plan of action to reach his goal. Motivation, to be self-sustaining, must be self-generated."

"Why should people be interested in motivation?" she asked.

"Because motivation is the basis for all constructive human behavior and achievement. High achievers use it to reach their objectives, to get things done that are important to them. Motivation incites action towards fulfillment, rather than procrastination or mere contemplation. Have you ever met a successful person who wasn't motivated?

*

MOTIVATION

IS THE BASIS

FOR ALL CONSTRUCTIVE

HUMAN BEHAVIOR AND

ACHIEVEMENT.

*

"Motivation can result only when you know what you want and you go after it with total conviction.

"The entire question of success in life really hinges on only two things -- your natural ability, and the depth and strength of your desires."

"Is it true that before you can hope to motivate others, you first must be motivated yourself?" she inquired.

"Absolutely. You may have met people who try to motivate others with outer charm but who lack inner conviction. It's like the shine on an apple which is only skin deep."

"But how can we acquire it?" she continued. "This seems so difficult."

"It really isn't," he suggested. "Essentially, it involves adopting certain attitudes and personality traits that facilitate goal achievement. Effective people need effective personalities, since effective personalities are essential to establish and maintain effective human relationships.

"First, let me explain what I mean by attitude and personality.

"Your mental attitude is your way of thinking. It shows your disposition, and opinions or beliefs about yourself and your life in general.

"Your personality is the outward expression of these inner attitudes and feelings.

"In other words, how you behave outwardly is a direct result of how you think and feel inwardly.

"Now, here are some identifiable personality attributes that all highly motivated people seem to possess.

"First, they have a healthy self-image and know their strengths and weaknesses. They have a quiet confidence in who they are and what they are capable of doing.

"They appear in control of themselves and accept full responsibility for their actions. Whether they succeed or not, they accept the results as a direct consequence of their behavior.

"They also display a positive approach to life in what they say and do. They see the good even in the bad. They don't avoid reality, they simply believe that optimism is more productive than pessimism.

"Motivated people are good two-way communicators and take 100% responsibility for both sending and receiving messages. They show genuine interest in other people and respect for their point-of-view.

"They practice being assertive in a positive way. They are not afraid to say who they are, what they think, and how they feel. This characterizes an active rather than passive approach to life.

"And they are committed people who persevere towards their goal. They are willing to pay the price to get the results they want. Roadblocks for them are only minor set-backs en route. High achievers always keep the end result firmly in mind.

"Finally, motivated people believe in the 'giving' way of life as opposed to the 'taking.' They put the spirit behind the Golden Rule into practice: give unto others those things you would have others give unto you, be it acceptance, praise, courtesy, goodwill or respect. They find that by 'giving' first, 'getting' takes care of itself.

"My advice to those who want to get excited about life is to get to know yourself and what you love to do. Find yourself a challenge, something you are genuinely interested in, then actively indulge in that passion with all the energy at your command."

"Now that you mention it," the young journalist interjected, "that's how I feel about motivation. There is nothing in the world I'm more interested in."

At this point, she looked pensive. "We know people can't change very easily. Are there some tools available to help?"

"Of course. You may already know we register thoughts in our mind in three dimensions. There is an idea component, an image component, and an emotional component. If we want to adopt a new idea, let's say a new, positive belief about ourselves, we have to become comfortable with the new idea first, then imagine being that kind of person in every detail, and finally experience the emotion associated with the new belief throughout our body.

"Take a baseball player who wants to become a better hitter. First, he must become comfortable with the idea that he can be a better hitter, then begin to imagine himself acting out this role in his imagination. The batter who 'sees' himself swinging the bat and hitting the ball into center field is more likely to get a hit than the batter who 'sees' himself striking out. Finally, the hitter must feel the excitement and exhilaration of getting this imaginary hit throughout his body as though he was actually hitting the ball in a real game.

"If you want to be successful at anything, you first have to be able to imagine it in every detail and firmly believe you can do it. As some perceptive person once said -- 'Whether you believe you can do a thing or not, you are right!'

"The process is not very revolutionary, though, since we have all done it before as children. We played 'let's pretend' and became whoever we wanted on command. We can adopt a new personality trait by decree -- simple say, "I want it, now I've got it!' You literally take possession of it and put it on display.

"I believe we become the person we spend the most time being each day. Like any good painter, we can dream our picture, then paint our dream to get the results we want. Similarly , we need only act out the role we want to assume in life."

"We're such creatures of habit and like to avoid risks. Is there something specific we can be doing each day to help us change gradually?" she asked.

"You're very perceptive," the master motivator offered. "The best way to bring about gradual change in behavior with minimal risk is to change what we say when we talk to ourselves all the time, sometimes at the rate of 1300 words per minute. Some call this 'self-talk' or our inner voice. Too often we are our own worst enemy by being overly critical. We put ourselves down because we aren't meeting standards compared to other people. We forget we

*

WE BECOME THE PERSON

WE SPEND THE MOST TIME

BEING EACH DAY.

*

can't be good at everything and should only be concerned with improving on our own past performance. Inner values and sense of purpose are the only sensible yardsticks. A person trying to succeed is not in competition with others -- he is only in competition with himself."

"Incredible. We are the product of our inner thoughts. I didn't know they were so important." The young journalist remained in deep thought.

The master motivator paused, then went on. "Words we say to ourselves with conviction are like fingers that mould our mind. Consider this. Each of us today is exactly where the sum total of all our inner thoughts and actions have brought us. We are now where we deserve to be, and we'll be at the same place tomorrow unless we decide we want to be somewhere else."

"That's a little scary," she commented. "You're saying it's our choice, that we are ultimately responsible for our own success."

*

IT'S OUR CHOICE.

WE ARE ULTIMATELY

RESPONSIBLE FOR OUR

OWN SUCCESS.

*

"Yes. Would you have it any other way?

"We know no one starts life with any of the necessary qualities and characteristics fully developed in order to succeed. If left to chance, we will develop some naturally enroute, some sooner, some later, and some never. But it doesn't have to be this way. We have control over this process if we choose to act."

The young journalist had a serious look on her face.

"I see," she said, "so it is possible to change, to think differently, and begin expanding our horizons -- but it helps to have our own built-in cheering section inside us constantly urging us on!"

She was smiling broadly.

The master motivator couldn't help but chuckle.

5

THE THIRD MEETING

The ideal working climate is where people mutually motivate one another.

I

The young journalist had come a long way in her thinking.

She had finally met a master motivator and been exposed to the greatest motivational concept in the world. She knew it would change her life.

She also understood what motivation really was and how to acquire it for herself.

Now she wanted to know more about how to apply G-M-C in organizational settings.

America was in trouble. Foreign products were dominating every market sector. From the TV set in the family room to the car in the garage, products from abroad were prominently on display.

What were we doing wrong?

More importantly, what were foreign manufacturers doing right?

She knew the master motivator could help her address these questions.

"Hello again," she said enthusiastically. "I hope we can continue."

"For as long as you like," he replied. "Time spent on process is always productive."

"I'd like to know how G-M-C applies to organizations and business. It seems to me that if we applied it correctly, we would be much more efficient in how we use our people resources to produce goods and services."

"Precisely. Understanding and proper application of G-M-C work to everyone's advantage. The manager wins, the employee wins, the customer wins, and the organization wins as well. Everyone's needs are satisfied if G-M-C is working as it should."

"This is very impressive. We have everything to gain and nothing to lose!" she volunteered. "It's so simple a concept."

"It certainly is. Unfortunately, people have difficulty accepting profound truths unless they are complex. G-M-C is important in business because productivity is the bottom line on profits. Without profits, a firm slowly dies."

"Productivity. Bottom line. Profits. I can't put all these into context," the young journalist admitted. "How are they linked?"

"In this way. Productivity translates into better price, quality, delivery and service. All of these reflect consumer wants and needs. Any firm providing a product or service must be sensitive to consumer preferences if it wants to stay in business."

"Are we failing to close the loop in some significant way?" she wondered.

"Only in this way. It's **people who determine both productivity and profits.** One group produces the product while another group consumes it.

"The question is, is everyone winning in the process? Are needs being met both in the workplace and in the marketplace? Let's break for coffee, then we'll look at the needs of employees in the workplace."

II

The master motivator continued. "Managers today are asking themselves a very important question -- 'Are industry and government organizations paying enough attention to individual motivation and quality of supervision on the job?' They believe these are two areas where increases in productivity can be readily achieved but are often overlooked.

"We know an organization develops its own personality through the attitudes of managerial-supervisory staff. I'm sure you've noticed that every organization has a different atmosphere, its own management style that sets the mood. A hospital or bank are not run like a pizza parlor, for example. This 'management style' is very important -- it puts on display for assessment how the organization goes about achieving its goals.

"On the other side of the equation, we have employees whose attitudes are important as well. Employee attitudes are a significant factor regarding the success or failure of managerial performance."

"Of course," the young journalist joined in. "Supervisors relating with employees and employees relating with supervisors. And each one of these relationships between an immediate supervisor and an employee adds up to either high or low morale for the organization as a whole."

"Very good!" he responded. "Many don't appreciate this simple fact. The well-being of any organization is only the sum of all the one-on-one relationships between each supervisor and each employee in the workplace. Effective interpersonal relationships on the job ensure improved staff relations, lower staff turnover, less absenteeism, higher productivity, and increased profits.

"The human relationship between each employee and his supervisor is critical. A well-run company is dependent on both individual and group initiatives for innovation and creativity. When G-M-C is applied correctly, the individual employee is utilized to the fullest extent possible of his creative and productive capacity."

*

THE WELL-BEING

OF ANY ORGANIZATION

IS ONLY THE SUM OF ALL THE

ONE-ON-ONE RELATIONSHIPS

BETWEEN EACH SUPERVISOR

AND EACH EMPLOYEE IN

THE WORK-PLACE.

*

The young woman now saw how pieces of the puzzle fit together. "People act in their own self-interest. The trick for the organization is to make this self-interest compatible with its own as much as possible. To get what it wants, the organization must ensure employees first get what they want."

"Terrific!" the gentleman beamed. "We're making great progress. A supervisor who tries to motivate an employee based on external rewards will quickly run out of dollars. He can pay a person only so much, whether it is a salary, a bonus, or a stock option plan. If he wants to be successful, he must appeal to the employee's inner needs and values, his sense of self-worth and self-respect. An organization stands to benefit to a significant degree if it can get people to drive **themselves**, since high level motivation produces high level results."

The journalist was reflecting on his last remark. "Motivating people then ... it simply helping others to motivate themselves. To be self-sustaining, the momentum must be self-generated."

"Absolutely. People need to be told when they are doing well, that their performance is commendable. You have to reward performance if performance is what you want. The ability to reward is a manager's most valuable tool."

The young journalist was impressed. "The first step in motivating others is to be motivated yourself, then set the proper example."

"That's right," the master motivator replied. "How we look, what we do, what we say, and how we say it, all have their effect. The way a supervisor relates to his staff is critical. An effective supervisor isn't afraid to hold regular staff meetings and ask -- 'How am I doing, as your boss?'

"During one-on-one encounters, he also explores with each employee what would help motivate him on the job. For one, it may be a corner office, for another a paid night course or the ability to leave the office early on Friday afternoons. Some employees would appreciate most a

*

YOU

HAVE TO REWARD

PERFORMANCE

IF

PERFORMANCE

IS WHAT YOU WANT

*

financial inducement in the form of a bonus at Christmas or just before summer vacation.

"The point is, the effective supervisor doesn't just guess the basic motivators of his staff. He seeks them out and tries to deliver -- for the benefit of the employee and the organization alike. He shows he cares."

"But all employees have different levels of experience and motivation," she continued. "Isn't this important?"

"It certainly is. A supervisor's managerial style must be an effective 'influencing' process. It has to take into account each individual's unique qualifications and experience.

"For example, a delegating style of management with minimal supervision may work fine for a highly motivated, experienced employee whereas a directing style with close supervision may be most appropriate for a promising newcomer who lacks experience.

"If the employee lacks both motivation and experience, he may need close support and supervision.

"An effective supervisor recognizes these needs by knowing his people. He then adopts the appropriate management style to get the results everyone wants. He aims for a 'win-win' situation."

A phone call for the master motivator interrupted the session. "That was the Chamber," he said. "The hall will be full tonight. I hope you're planning to attend."

"I'm looking forward to it very much," she said.

And she was.

III

The master motivator had just returned to his chair.

"Let's analyze the process in the organization a little more closely," he suggested, "and look at 'management by objectives.' Organizations exist because they alone can achieve goals their individual members cannot. An organization must strive to focus through some mechanism the efforts, talents and energies of all their employees towards value goals and objectives consistent with the organization's well-being. Both employees and the organization must know where they want to go if they want to end up in the same place."

The young journalist was turning yet another page in her notebook. She wrote 'goal setting' at the top.

"Yes" she observed, "a manager's main responsibility is to get results with and through his people. As you said, these results represent the organization's bottom line -- essentially the list of major corporate goals."

"That's the process," he said. "'Management by objectives' is a form of planning and control that motivates managers and employees alike by creating personal goals that are mutually agreed upon. Of course, any system is only as effective as the people who design and use it. It should be a relatively simple process to measure and improve personal performance and ensure that objectives are consistent throughout the organization.

"By using 'management by objectives,' a firm can satisfy employee demands for greater involvement in decision-making and goal-setting. It encourages two-way communications, thus increasing cooperation and commitment among staff to achieve goals they have set for themselves. A good planning system allows communication of the firm's objectives up and down the organization's structure."

"You are saying that goal setting is a key aspect in the supervisor-employee relationship. Can you give an example?"

"Delighted," the master motivator replied. "Let's look at America's favorite sport. Have you ever wondered why baseball players and baseball fans are so excited about their game?

"The game centers around home plate where the batter knows exactly what he is trying to do -- get a hit and run to first base. He knows this is his goal, his team manager knows this is his goal, and all the players and fans know it. During the course of a game, the batter expects three or four turns at bat and understands that he has three strikes on each occasion to get a hit. When he succeeds, everyone notices and everyone cheers. This positive reinforcement of his ability to succeed spurs him on to keep trying no matter how many times he strikes out. Although the umpire may shout 'three strikes, you're out!' he says 'three strikes, I win because I'll be back!'

"The batter is automatically motivated by his environment, in this case the baseball stadium, to concentrate on his successes instead of his failures. Confidence is built upon the experience of success.

*

CONFIDENCE

IS BUILT UPON

THE EXPERIENCE OF

SUCCESS.

*

"Now put yourself in the position of the immediate 'supervisor-pitcher.' You are throwing the pitches and you are in control of the complexity of the game for your 'employee-batter.'

"First you make sure he knows all the rules of the game and what he should be concentrating on. Work with him in writing these down and have him agree with them.

"You now begin the game by throwing the pitches sure and true, straight over home plate -- but don't throw any fast balls, curve balls or low balls. Aim for consistency and fair play. You want him to succeed, you want him to concentrate on his successes, and you want him to be self-motivated for his own good and that of the organization. Your objective is to get this person so comfortable with 'getting hits' that he expects to be successful all the time. As you see him succeed, your own success is reinforced as well because you are accomplishing something good as a teacher. Most people have to be taught how to be successful in life.

"As the game begins, you may throw a few bad

pitches, unintentionally of course, and your 'employee-batter' will giggle in delight. He notices his boss isn't perfect. But you both are really laughing a bit at each other because, at first, your 'employee-batter' will be a lousy hitter as well.

"Your job is to make him more comfortable at the plate and to point out constructively what he's doing wrong so he can succeed. In this way, you'll both be part of an effective team. A supervisor can elicit the teamwork he needs only by being a team player himself.

"Whether in life or in sports, people will do what you want them to do -- not so much because they have to, but because they want to. When you show an individual that he'll gain what he longs for the most -- recognition, acceptance, self-respect, then help him achieve it, he'll always perform at his best."

*

A

SUPERVISOR CAN

ELICIT THE TEAMWORK

HE NEEDS ONLY BY

BEING A

TEAM PLAYER

HIMSELF.

*

IV

The young journalist didn't know there was so much to be learned from the game of baseball.

"Fantastic. That takes us to your final point," she noted. "You were going to address G-M-C and how it applies to the needs of people in the marketplace."

"Yes, we must close the loop," he agreed. "Have you heard the expression -- 'There is no better customer than a satisfied customer?' We know satisfied customers are repeat customers. No product lasts forever.

"People may want to buy what you have to sell but they also need to feel important. They don't care how much you know about your product or service until they know how much you care about helping them solve their problem. When you show people that their problem is important to you, they'll be as anxious to buy from you as you are to sell to them. The salesperson who has developed the habit of making other people feel important is creating a receptive, buying attitude.

"The selling business is the people business. Research shows that 85% of successful selling is based on **people skills** and only 15% on **product knowledge.** When it comes to sales training, most organizations reverse these figures. They simply assume most people already know how to initiate and maintain effective human relationships, when in reality they don't. This is especially important when you realize that 81% of all new jobs in America will be in the service sector."

"You have a strong message there," the young journalist noted.

"Yes. One of my principal goals is to expose this fact and get American business back on track."

The master motivator exhibited a quiet confidence and stoic determination that was very impressive. He seemed like a man possessed with a mission in life, with a strong belief in this work.

V

"Let's sum up," he suggested. "We can see that the organization must satisfy the needs of its employees in the workplace. And the organization must satisfy the needs of its customers in the marketplace. Both lead to increased productivity and higher profits.

"The well-being of our whole economy is based on the free enterprise system. Individual initiative, creativity and ingenuity all contribute to new investment and the means of production.

"The laws of supply and demand, and survival of the fittest control the marketplace, and people are free to find their niche within the system and seek out the rewards it offers.

"People are encouraged to apply their individual talents and energies towards the accumulation of wealth in open competition with others, each in pursuit of his own dream.

"Too often firms have lost sight of their reason for being. The secret of success in business is to find a need and fill it. Unless your product or service is directed at helping people solve their problem, you will not succeed in the long run.

"In a free society, people will patronize you only if you have their interests in mind.

"The free enterprise system is based on natural laws of human behavior, and generally rewards those who contribute the most to society."

The young journalist sat back as he finished. The master motivator had explained a great deal and shown just how important G-M-C was in business in America today. She guessed few people really understood what she had just learned.

*

IN A FREE

SOCIETY, PEOPLE

WILL PATRONIZE YOU

ONLY IF YOU HAVE

THEIR INTERESTS

IN MIND.

*

6

THE FOURTH MEETING

A child needs encouragement just as a flower needs nourishment and sunshine.

The last meeting was arranged for 6 p.m.

The woman wondered what additional information she needed for her research.

One area seemed untouched. Children. The next generation, our future leaders.

Were we, as adults, doing all we could to teach our children to function effectively? Were we setting the proper example?

She decided to seek the views of the master motivator on the matter, to explore with him how G-M-C, the greatest motivational concept in the world, could be used to establish effective relationships between adults and children.

The gentleman was already dressed for his speaking engagement later in the evening.

He looked superb.

"Well," he smiled, "you seem eager to begin our last session."

"Yes. I'd like to talk about children and family relationships," she said. "In your opinion, what is the role of the family in our modern society?"

"Children first learn the vital art of getting along with other people through family membership. The heart of family life lies in how individual family members relate with one another.

"The real value of family in today's changing world is in the acceptance, security and understanding of its members. Children can overcome many difficulties when they are secure in their family relationships and their shared affection is one of life's principal sources of happiness."

"Is the family still a viable institution?" she asked.

"I believe it is. People need to belong and have close personal relationships with others. The family best serves this purpose if it is properly structured and if its members are willing to sacrifice some of their personal freedom for the good of the whole. The family has the unique ability to define and develop group goals which individual members alone cannot achieve."

"How do you bring about this spirit of cooperation and compromise?" she asked.

"It's by establishing effective human relationships. Parents know the principal concern of child-rearing is personality formulation and character development. They have to set the proper example, and teach the spirit of cooperation and compromise.

"Children are unique in their needs. Very often, we have to sell children on these needs rather than on their wants.

"For example, we know at some point in their upbringing, children will have to commit themselves to a particular life-style and assume full responsibility for all their decisions. The successful family will turn out young adults who are able to respond and function effectively to challenges in their environment. Dynamic parents will pass on to their children the necessary desire, interest and skills such that they will find meaning to their existence, even perform a job that has yet to be invented."

"Traditional methods of child-rearing have changed," the woman noted. "Autocratic parents who only make demands on their children are failing to get the desired results. What are they doing wrong?"

"The trend towards more individual freedom in our liberated society has had a significant impact on family relationships. It requires more human awareness, understanding and mutual respect. The modern family is faced with the difficult task of trying to maintain the ideals, standards and practices found valid in the past, while at the same time having to adopt new beliefs and behavior considered acceptable today."

The woman agreed. "But young people still need rules to help guide them and criteria to judge themselves and their behavior. Are you saying adults not in tune with children's perceptions and expectations will have a difficult time providing this valuable assistance?"

"Of course. But it must work both ways. Children do not always understand that increased freedom necessarily requires respect for the rights of others in return for exercising their own rights.

"Some children believe only they have rights and only adults have responsibilities. On the other hand, adults often forget that the arbitrary reward-punishment technique for controlling children's behavior is no longer valid. Children do not accept that age and experience alone are relevant factors in their relationships with adults. Clearly alternate methods must be found if individual motivation and morale are to be fostered and directed towards more productive and meaningful goals."

"Enter the greatest motivational concept in the world," the young journalist announced.

"I knew you'd have the answer!" the gentleman exclaimed.

II

"We should all expect children to misbehave. It is integral to their development," he went on. "Unfortunately, we often pay undue attention to this misbehavior, forgetting that the majority of their actions and activities are appropriate, even commendable. Too often we practice destructive criticism when we should be practicing deserving praise.

"The primary objective of each and every encounter between an adult and a child is to enhance the child's sense of self-esteem. It is the greatest gift you can give your child. Parents and teachers alike need to be sensitive to this, and separate negative feelings about misbehavior from a child to protect his ego, and transfer positive feelings to a child on appropriate occasions to foster his ego. We must allow children to benefit from their childhood experiences instead of being impeded by them. It takes a long time to undo a negative self-image once it is set in concrete!"

*

TOO OFTEN WE

PRACTICE DESTRUCTIVE

CRITICISM WHEN WE SHOULD

BE PRACTICING

DESERVING

PRAISE.

*

The woman was nodding her head in agreement. She could relate his comments to her own childhood experiences.

"Without mistakes, there is no discovery. A child's misbehavior should never be linked to his own sense of self-worth," she said softly.

"Precisely. How adults respond to misbehavior is the critical part of the encounter. Because of their maturity, adults are in a better position to function rationally when relating to children. They should know what they are doing, why they are doing it, and with some certainty the results they will achieve. It contrasts with emotional, responsive behavior that is spontaneous and often ill-considered. Adults need to understand that children see through different eyes, then try to identify with this other frame of reference.

"Acting rather than reacting allows you to maintain control and use what you have learned. It provides the opportunity to modify misbehavior in a positive and constructive way. Consultation rather than confrontation should always be the objective."

*

CONSULTATION

RATHER THAN

CONFRONTATION

SHOULD

ALWAYS BE

THE OBJECTIVE

*

"How can adults help children establish a healthy self-image?" she asked.

"In many ways. For example, it can be nurtured and fostered through an open exchange and verbal transfer of values and attributes in conversation. Mom's statement, 'Catherine, I'm so proud of you' to her daughter is not as effective as saying, 'You must be very proud of yourself, Catherine,' in order to instill excitement and positive feelings. Direct verbal transfers help instill desire and motivation within a child to excel through trial and error, and individual effort. Mother is also allowing her child to satisfy her own ego needs in a more personalized way by experiencing herself the emotional uplift and stimulation that follows achievement.

"Another way is to practice truly unconditional love. Explain to your children that no matter what they do, you will always love them. Although there will be occasions when they may disobey you and have to be punished, tell them that this will not interfere with your total love for them as a person. By your example, show your children that their behavior will never result in the withholding of love from them.

"And a father can instill in his son a sense of adventure in life through positive expectations. He can say each morning, 'David, it's going to be a terrific day today and good things will happen to you.' Invariably, some good things happen every day, and the child will be expecting them and recognize them immediately. Such events will then take on a greater significance in his reality structure. His son will be learning to expect and anticipate good things to happen regularly."

"I like these!" the woman said with delight. "But invariably there are confrontations. How does a parent handle these?"

"You compare wants and needs, and give first then take," he offered. "Assume your child wants to go to a rock concert but not do her homework. As her mother, you want her to do her homework but are flexible about the concert. So the child's want and your want are clear. But the relevant factors to be considered are the child's need to do well in school, to succeed academically in order to make something of her life, and your need to feel that you are acting as a responsible parent.

"In this case, you must help the child see that it is in her own self-interest to do her homework, that the gain to be had is hers, not yours. When you do this with sincerity and a spirit of compromise, you can agree to the child's request to go out as a reward for her seeing and agreeing to what is only in her own self-interest anyway."

"To the extent I give others what they want, they will give me what I want in return." The journalist repeated these words as she was underlining them in her notebook.

"But what have I, as the parent, given first?" she inquired with a puzzled look on her face.

"With soft touches and a warm smile, I would say genuine affection," he replied, "and focused attention with direct eye contact. By your behavior, the child knows you care. Parents need to act out their role as teacher and counselor in an atmosphere of sincerity, moderation, humility and love."

*

PARENTS NEED TO ACT

OUT THEIR ROLE AS TEACHER

AND COUNSELOR IN AN ATMOSPHERE

OF SINCERITY, MODERATION,

HUMILITY AND LOVE.

*

7

SAYING GOODBYE

To be a teacher ... to teach others how to help themselves, must surely be considered a noble task.

It was over.

After four meetings with the master motivator, it was time to leave.

She was tingling with excitement inside. What she had learned stirred her emotions.

"I'm very grateful to you," she said solemnly. "I don't know how I can ever repay you for all the time and wisdom you've shared with me."

"You get to keep and enjoy what you share and give away," he commented. "I know you'll do the same. What a person knows and believes should find expression in what he does.

"If you know how to get things done with and through other people in a spirit of joy and harmony, and help them grow as people in the process, then you possess one of the most treasured talents in the world. You are needed. And you will be rewarded in many ways."

The woman was unable to respond.

He put his arm around her and walked towards the door.

"No person is ever honored for what he receives. Honor is bestowed only on those who give. By giving of yourself, you help create something larger than yourself. It's in our self-interest to help one another.

"We are told -- 'To whom much is given, much shall be required.' Motivation and success are not only a reward to be enjoyed, they are a sacred trust to be shared. I have given them to you."

The master motivator was about to begin his speech. His title was "G-M-C, THE GREATEST MOTIVATIONAL CONCEPT IN THE WORLD."

"Good evening, ladies and gentlemen.

"I'm very pleased to be here, and I want to congratulate you on coming out tonight.

"Like you, I believe the most profitable investment in the world any of us can make is an investment in ourselves. By that I mean, before real estate, stocks, bonds or commodities, you and the attitudes you adopt will ultimately decide your fate and determine your relative success in life.

The master motivator went on to introduce his revolutionary concept.

In any relationship, you must first give others what they want before you can expect to receive what you want in return.

"The application of G-M-C ought to be part of our everyday life since it is the answer to many of our personal, parental, and professional business problems.

"It is generally agreed that the most dominant need in human nature is a craving for recognition. People actively seek out approval, appreciation and acceptance in everything they say and do. We all want to feel important. It is an instinctive, driving force in our make-up. Yet, ironically, we do not spend enough time giving to others what we are desperately seeking for ourselves.

"Recognition is a psychological ingredient as vital to a hungry ego as nourishment is to an empty stomach. Without regular replenishment of both, the human system's ability to function breaks down. We all want others to acknowledge that as individuals we are important and that what we do is worthwhile.

"The need to show respect and to give praise is wisdom that has been passed down to us for centuries. Few would expect that today, late in the 20th century, we are still failing to heed this valuable advice, leading to inefficiencies, even turmoil, in our homes, schools and modern factories.

"Where does this leave us, then?

"It was discovered early on that 'a fair day's work for a fair day's pay' resulted in only 'fair' production. To improve productivity, behavioral psychologists and management experts began to experiment with various motivational techniques such as the proposition that 'more pay equals better work.' They soon discovered, however, that it was valid only up to a point. After basic financial needs were satisfied, they found that worker productivity again levelled off. Like food or water, money was of the essence only when it was in short supply.

"So what could the elixir be?

"It seems that each of us has been endowed with a hierarchy of human needs and wants. In progressing order, they are:

LEVEL I

- physiological needs/wants: food, air, rest, sex, shelter, other bodily functions and protection from the elements

LEVEL II

- safety needs/wants: freedom from fear, protection against danger, threat and deprivation

LEVEL III

- social needs/wants: affiliation, association, acceptance, friendship and love

LEVEL IV

- ego needs/wants: recognition, pride, status, appreciation, achievement and self-respect

LEVEL V

- self-actualization needs/wants: high achievement, competence, creativity and a degree of personal autonomy

"People naturally seek out satisfaction at Levels IV and V, for example, after all needs/wants in the first three levels have been met.

"The answer, then, can be found by observing what all people want the most after their desire for basic health, safety, and social needs have been met. In a word, it is the need to feel important, to have a sort of intellectual acknowledgement of their self-worth.

"People who are wealthy, for example, all want to be 'recognized' by the world as Very Important People, whether it's an honorary title or a concert hall named after them.

"Now we know what other people want from us; and we know that to get people to do what we want, we must give them what they want first.

"Certainly consumer advertising has applied this knowledge successfully in their television commercials. Before we walk through their door, a muffler company tells us, 'You're a somebody!' And a hamburger chain says, 'We do it all for you!' Even a shampoo manufacturer, who wants to help you look your very best, states up front, 'And you're worth it!'

"What can we all do as individuals, then, to achieve our goals with and through other people?

"First, we must recognize that unlike our desire to receive, which is a natural instinct, the desire to give is something we must all learn.

"Second, we must understand that it is not a question of 'givers' being the good guys and 'takers' being the bad guys -- it is a matter of being effective.

"Third, we must appreciate that total givers do not purposely go about 'getting' anything -- yet they do receive in great abundance.

"So begin to practice being a total giver regularly, giving ego gratification to help motivate other people to go in the direction you want. Give sincerely, consistently and in proportion to the deed -- but foremost, always remember to give, and to give first.

"In conclusion, I'd like to issue a challenge to you. For the next week, try to predict the daily encounters you are going to have and how you want them to go. Then visualize clearly in your mind these encounters going well and assume you will get the results you want. Put G-M-C into practice.

"It is a universal law ... when you give other people something they desperately need and want first, you'll always get what you want in return. 'Giving' is the only 'how to' lesson you'll ever need to learn in this world -- and it will help you when you are about to enter the next.

"Think back in time, and you'll see the world never forgets the greatest givers in history, those who left behind something greater than themselves. Who hasn't heard of and admired them all -- Dr. Albert Schweitzer, Mother Teresa of Calcutta and Jesus of Nazareth. They all believed that to act in the service of others was the secret source of true peace and lifelong satisfaction ...."

As the master motivator concluded his speech, the young journalist remembered the gentleman's kindness and knew how much he cared for people.

Her eyes became misty as she remembered his challenge -- sharing, sharing, sharing.

He was sharing. She had yet to begin.

She got up and quietly left the hall.

Her research was done. She had to get started. She could begin to write her book now.

It would be titled -- **THE GREATEST MOTIVATIONAL CONCEPT IN THE WORLD.**

This book has no end, it can only be used
as a beginning. It is dedicated to all
progressive thinkers, dreamers, and doers.
The future is truly in their hands.

HISTORICAL REFERENCES

The concept of giving as a philosophy of life is as old as history itself.

- Zoroaster taught it in Persia three thousand years ago ....
- Confucius preached it in China two thousand five hundred years ago ....
- Buddha counseled it in India two thousand four hundred years ago ...
- Jesus proposed it in Judea almost two thousand years ago ....

BIBLICAL REFERENCES

- "Whatever a man sows, that will he also reap." (Galatians 6:7)
- "Cast your bread upon the waters, for you will find it after many days." (Ecclesiastes 11:1)
- "The measure you give will be the measure you get." (Matthew 7:2)
- "He who would be greatest among you must first be servant of all." (Mark 9:35)

CLASSIC BOOK REFERENCES

Allen, James. AS A MAN THINKETH. New York: Gosset and Dunlap, Inc., 1959.

Bach, Richard. JONATHON LIVINGSTON SEAGULL. Macmillian Publishing Company, 1970.

Bristol, Claude. THE MAGIC OF BELIEVING. Engelwood Cliffs, N.J.: Prentice-Hall, Inc. 1957.

Carnegie, Dale. HOW TO WIN FRIENDS AND INFLUENCE PEOPLE. New York: Simon and Shuster, Inc., 1936.

Conwell, Russell. ACRES OF DIAMONDS. Hallmark Cards, Inc., 1968.

Dyer, Wayne. THE SKY'S THE LIMIT. Simon and Shuster, Inc., 1980.

Hill, Napoleon. THINK AND GROW RICH. New York: Hawthorne Books, Inc., 1966.

Lorayne, Harry. SECRETS OF MIND POWER. Frederick Fell, Inc., 1961.

Maltz, Maxwell, M.D. PSYCHO-CYBERNETICS: THE NEW WAY TO A SUCCESSFUL LIFE. Englewood Cliffs, N.J.: Prentice-Hall, Inc., 1960.

Newman, James. RELEASE YOUR BRAKES. Warner Communications, 1977.

Peale, Norman Vincent. THE POWER OF POSITIVE THINKING. Prentice-Hall, Inc., 1956.

Schuller, Robert. THE PEAK TO PEAK PRINCIPLE. Doubleday and Company, 1980.

Schwartz, David. THE MAGIC OF THINKING BIG. Simon and Schuster, 1959.

Waitley, Denis. SEEDS OF GREATNESS. Simon and Schuster, 1983.

"Before renewing the systems, the institutions and the methods, one must seek renewal at the heart of man first ...."

Jean - Paul II